SCHOLASTIC
READ&RESPOND

Bringing the best books to life in the classroom

Activities based on Letters from the Lighthouse
By Emma Carroll

Emma Carroll

LETTERS
FROM THE
LIGHTHOUSE

'Like Michael Morpurgo and Philip Pullman, Carroll . . . knows she can keep her listeners in thrall.' *Telegraph*

FOR AGES 7–11

Published in the UK by Scholastic Education, 2020
Scholastic Distribution Centre, Bosworth Avenue, Tournament Fields, Warwick, CV34 6UQ
Scholastic Ireland, 89E Lagan Road, Dublin Industrial Estate, Glasnevin, Dublin, D11 HP5F

SCHOLASTIC and associated logos are trademarks and/or registered trademarks of Scholastic Inc.

www.scholastic.co.uk

© 2020 Scholastic

3 4 5 6 7 8 9 4 5 6 7 8 9 0 1 2 3
Printed and bound by Ashford Colour Press

This book is made of materials from well-managed,
FSC®-certified forests and other controlled sources.

A CIP catalogue record for this book is available from the British Library.
ISBN 978-1407-18325-1

Extracts from *The National Curriculum in England, English Programme of Study* © Crown Copyright. Reproduced under the terms of the Open Government Licence (OGL). http://www.nationalarchives.gov.uk/doc/open-government-licence/version/3

Authors Jillian Powell
Editorial team Rachel Morgan, Vicki Yates, Suzanne Adams, Julia Roberts
Series designers Dipa Mistry and Andrea Lewis
Typesetter QBS Learning
Illustrator Barry Ablett

Acknowledgements
The publishers gratefully acknowledge permission to reproduce the following copyright material: **Faber & Faber** for permission to use the cover from *Letters from the Lighthouse* written by Emma Carroll.

Photograph
Page 18: Coastal defences, Shutterstock

Every effort has been made to trace copyright holders for the works reproduced in this book, and the publishers apologise for any inadvertent omissions.

CONTENTS ▼

How to use Read & Respond in your classroom...   4

Curriculum links   6

About the book and the author   8

Guided reading   9

Shared reading   13

Grammar, punctuation & spelling   19

Plot, character & setting   25

Talk about it   32

Get writing   38

Assessment   44

How to use Read & Respond in your classroom...

Read & Respond provides teaching ideas related to a specific well-loved children's book. Each Read & Respond book is divided into the following sections:

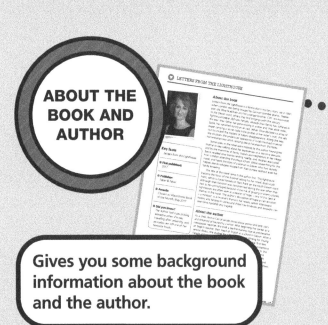

ABOUT THE BOOK AND AUTHOR

Gives you some background information about the book and the author.

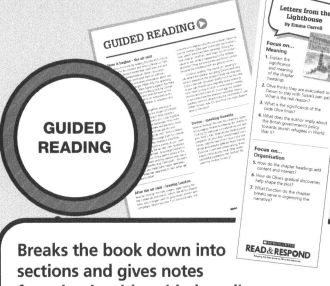

GUIDED READING

Breaks the book down into sections and gives notes for using it with guided reading groups. A bookmark has been provided on page 12 containing comprehension questions. The children can be directed to refer to these as they read.

SHARED READING

Provides extracts from the children's book with associated notes for focused work. There is also one non-fiction extract that relates to the children's book.

GRAMMAR, PUNCTUATION & SPELLING

Provides word-level work related to the children's book so you can teach grammar, punctuation and spelling in context.

PLOT, CHARACTER & SETTING

Contains activity ideas focused on the plot, characters and the setting of the story.

TALK ABOUT IT

Has speaking and listening activities related to the children's book. These activities may be based directly on the children's book or be broadly based on the themes and concepts of the story.

GET WRITING

Provides writing activities related to the children's book. These activities may be based directly on the children's book or be broadly based on the themes and concepts of the story.

ASSESSMENT

Contains short activities that will help you assess whether the children have understood concepts and curriculum objectives. They are designed to be informal activities to feed into your planning.

> **"** The titles are great fun to use and cover exactly the range of books that children most want to read. It makes it easy to explore texts fully and ensure the children want to keep on reading more. **"**
>
> *Chris Flanagan, Year 5 Teacher,*
> *St Thomas of Canterbury*
> *Primary School*

Activities

The activities follow the same format:

- **Objective:** the objective for the lesson. It will be based upon a curriculum objective, but will often be more specific to the focus being covered.

- **What you need:** a list of resources you need to teach the lesson, including photocopiable pages.

- **What to do:** the activity notes.

- **Differentiation:** this is provided where specific and useful differentiation advice can be given to support and/or extend the learning in the activity. Differentiation by providing additional adult support has not been included as this will be at a teacher's discretion based upon specific children's needs and ability, as well as the availability of support.

The activities are numbered for reference within each section and should move through the text sequentially – so you can use the lesson while you are reading the book. Once you have read the book, most of the activities can be used in any order you wish.

CURRICULUM LINKS

Section	Activity	Curriculum objectives
Guided reading		Comprehension: To understand what they read by checking that the book makes sense to them, discussing their understanding and exploring the meaning of words in context.
Shared reading	1	Comprehension: To discuss and evaluate how authors use language, including figurative language, considering the impact on the reader.
	2	Comprehension: To identify how language, structure and presentation contribute to meaning.
	3	Comprehension: To discuss and evaluate how authors use language, including figurative language, considering the impact on the reader.
	4	Comprehension: To understand what they read by checking the book makes sense to them, discussing their understanding and exploring the meaning of words in context; to retrieve information from non-fiction.
Grammar, punctuation & spelling	1	Vocabulary, grammar and punctuation: To use expanded noun phrases to convey complicated information concisely.
	2	Vocabulary, grammar and punctuation: To recognise vocabulary and structures that are appropriate for formal speech and writing, including subjunctive forms.
	3	Vocabulary, grammar and punctuation: To use modal verbs or adverbs to indicate degrees of possibility.
	4	Vocabulary, grammar and punctuation: To use the perfect forms of verbs to mark relationships of time and cause.
	5	Vocabulary, grammar and punctuation: To use passive verbs to affect the presentation of information in a sentence.
	6	Vocabulary, grammar and punctuation: To use relative clauses beginning with who, which, where, when, whose, that or an implied (ie omitted relative pronoun).
Plot, character & setting	1	Comprehension: To identify how language, structure and presentation contribute to meaning.
	2	Comprehension: To summarise the main ideas drawn from more than one paragraph, identifying key details that support the main ideas.
	3	Comprehension: To identify how language, structure and presentation contribute to meaning.
	4	Comprehension: To draw inferences such as inferring characters' feelings, thoughts and motives from their actions, and to justify inferences with evidence.
	5	Comprehension: To predict what might happen from details stated and implied; to identify how language, structure and presentation contribute to meaning.
	6	Comprehension: To ask questions to improve their understanding.
	7	Comprehension: To draw inferences such as inferring characters' feelings, thoughts and motives from their actions, and to justify inferences with evidence.
	8	Comprehension: To understand what they read by summarising the main ideas drawn from more than one paragraph, identifying key details that support the main ideas.

Section	Activity	Curriculum objectives
Talk about it	1	Spoken language: To maintain attention and participate actively in collaborative conversations, staying on topic and initiating and responding to comments.
	2	Spoken language: To use spoken language to develop understanding through speculating, hypothesising, imagining and exploring ideas.
	3	Spoken language: To use spoken language to develop understanding through speculating, hypothesising, imagining and exploring ideas.
	4	Spoken language: To use relevant strategies to build their vocabulary.
	5	Spoken language: To participate in discussions.
	6	Spoken language: To give well-structured descriptions; to participate in presentations.
Get writing	1	Composition: To identify the audience for and purpose of the writing, selecting the appropriate form and using other similar writing as models for their own.
	2	Composition: To plan their writing by considering how authors have developed characters and settings in what pupils have read.
	3	Comprehension: To discuss and evaluate how authors use language, including figurative language, considering the impact on the reader.
	4	Comprehension: To summarise the main ideas drawn from more than one paragraph.
	5	Composition: To draft and write by selecting appropriate grammar and vocabulary, understanding how such choices can change and enhance meaning; to perform their own compositions, using appropriate intonation and volume.
	6	Composition: To use organisational and presentational devices to structure text and guide the reader (for example, headings, bullet points, underlining).
Assessment	1	Vocabulary, grammar and punctuation: To use relative clauses beginning with who, which, where, when, whose or that.
	2	Comprehension: To summarise the main ideas drawn from more than one paragraph.
	3	Spoken language: To give well-structured descriptions, explanations and narratives for different purposes, including for expressing feelings.
	4	Comprehension: To summarise the main ideas drawn from more than one paragraph.
	5	Spoken language: To maintain attention and participate actively in collaborative conversations, staying on topic and initiating and responding to comments.
	6	Comprehension: To identify the audience for and purpose of the writing, selecting the appropriate form and using other similar writing as models for their own.

Key facts

Letters from the Lighthouse

⦿ **First published:**
2017

⦿ **Publisher:**
Faber & Faber

⦿ **Awards:**
Chosen as Waterstones Book of the Month, May 2017

⦿ **Did you know?**
The author had a job picking avocados when she was travelling after university, and avocados are still one of her favourite foods.

About the book

Letters from the Lighthouse is a World War II mystery story, set in 1941, when London was being ravaged by German bomber planes. Twelve-year-old Olive Bradshaw and her younger brother, Cliff, are evacuated to the Devon coast, where they find lodgings with the solitary lighthouse keeper, Ephraim Pengilly. Already their family has suffered in the war: their father has gone missing in action and their elder sister, Sukie, has vanished during an air raid. When Olive discovers a scrap of paper carrying a secret code in the pocket of her sister's coat, she sets out to unravel the mystery of Sukie's disappearance. Along the way, she discovers the undercover operations of locals involved in secret humanitarian war work rescuing Jewish families from the Nazis.

Some ideas in the novel were inspired by the author hearing her mother-in-law talking about her experiences as a wartime evacuee, and by the memories of family, friends and neighbours in her village. Some recalled stray bombs landing nearby, and children evacuated from London attending the village school. While researching for the novel, she heard the story of a woman in Devon who had secretly helped Jewish refugees escape from Nazi Europe without even her family knowing.

The title of the novel came to the author first. The lighthouse became the focus of the fictional setting for her novel, Budmouth Point, which is based loosely on Start Point on the south Devon coast. Although their function was compromised during the war when they had to be camouflaged because of the risk of guiding in enemy planes, lighthouses are often seen as a beacon of hope – one of the central themes in the novel. The author's description of hope as 'an emotion – a mindset', is a recurrent theme in her novels, which interweave history and fantasy in stories and show how kindness and empathy can overcome hardship and tragedy.

About the author

As a child, Emma Carroll wrote stories about ponies and pop stars and dreamed of becoming a writer. After beginning her career as a newspaper reporter, she took a teacher-training course and became an English teacher, then Head of English at a school in Devon. After a serious illness, she studied for a Master of Arts in Writing for Young People at Bath Spa University in 2009. The success of her first few novels encouraged her to become a full-time writer. She has become known as the Queen of Historical Fiction, for novels often set in the past, sometimes spooky, redolent with mystery and suspense and featuring feisty characters. *Letters from the Lighthouse* is her sixth novel. Emma Carroll lives in the Somerset hills with her husband and two 'talkative' Jack Russell terriers. She describes herself as a dog lover, bookworm and tea drinker.

GUIDED READING ▶

How it begins – the air raid

Introduce the book by reading the title and looking for clues to the content and setting (Britain in 1941, during the Second World War; child evacuees and a mysterious disappearance). Before you begin reading, establish some brief facts on context, inviting children to volunteer information about the war: when it was fought (1939–45), the opposing sides (Britain and her Allies fighting against Germany and her Allies), and how bombing raids by German planes on British towns and cities (known as 'the Blitz') meant children had to be evacuated to the countryside. Encourage children to volunteer any family links to the war.

Read the first chapter together, pausing to note the title, which quotes the slogan of a British government campaign aiming to keep people's spirits up ('Keep calm and carry on'). Look together at questions 1 and 5 on the bookmark. Then refer to question 8 on the bookmark and pause to check that the children understand war-specific and period-specific vocabulary ('air raid', 'Picture Palace', 'Luftwaffe', 'telegram'). Encourage them to consider how war has impacted the children's lives (their father has been killed; food is scarce). As you read the passage describing the air raid, raise questions 9 and 10 on the bookmark. Encourage children to think about the effect of the capital letters in the screen announcement and the capitals with italics used when the bombs drop (*'WHUMP', 'THUMP'*). Ask: *What do you think Sukie might have been doing and what has happened to her? What has happened to Olive?*

After the air raid – leaving London

Read on through the next chapter, again noting the title ('Make do and mend'), which, like all the chapter titles, was a slogan used for government posters and campaigns. Revisit question 5 on the bookmark. Ask

a volunteer to explain why the nurse thinks Olive has lost her mother (Olive was found with her mother's coat, which Sukie had been wearing). During the next chapter, 'Mothers: send them out of London', pause to ask: *What is happening to the children and why?* (They are being evacuated from London because the bombing raids are getting worse.)

Continue reading 'The round-up', pausing to ask where the children are going (Devon) and why Olive is pleased at the prospect (they will stay with Sukie's 'pen pal' Queenie). Briefly focus on the idea of pen pals (friends who regularly wrote letters to each other to stay in touch in times before mobile phones and the internet). Encourage the children to speculate how the evacuees would be feeling. (excited, nervous, afraid) Note the confrontation with Esther Jenkins. Ask: *Do you think she might feature later in the story?*

Devon – meeting Queenie

Read on through the next two chapters, again encouraging children to interpret the chapter titles ('Caring for evacuees is a national service' and 'Do your duty'). Ask: *What do you think a poster urging people to 'do your duty' would mean?* (serve in the forces; help the war effort) *How is the children's arrival at Queenie's different from their expectations?* (Queenie is cold and unwelcoming; there is no supper.) *Why do you think Olive writes such an untruthful postcard to her mother?* (She doesn't want her mother to worry.)

GUIDED READING

The Luftwaffe attack – the lighthouse awaits

As you read the next chapter, 'Lend a hand on the land', check that the children understand the idea of 'rationing' in wartime, when the government limited the amount of food and other goods in short supply that each person could buy. Ask: *Why do you think Mrs Drummond would return her bacon ration?* (The chicken she had requested replaced it – she could not have both.) Raise question 11 on the bookmark.

As you continue reading through the next three chapters, highlight terms familiar in the war, such as 'air-raid warden' and 'Jerry' (see question 8 on the bookmark). Ask a volunteer to explain how Cliff gets Sukie's phrase wrong at the beginning of 'Loose lips sink ships' (it should be 'the cat's pyjamas'). Pause after the second chapter break in 'Attack on all fronts' to ask: *Can you explain why Olive and Cliff must move out of Queenie's house?* (Queenie is the only one who will take Esther, and they can't be billeted together.) Read on and explore what they understand by the term 'Kindertransport' children? (They were Jewish children rescued from Germany and German-occupied countries such as Austria.)

A clue – a secret code

As you read on through 'Walls have ears', encourage the children to consider how the author builds suspense through the slow revealing of clues, which Olive is trying to piece together (the foreign map and code which she found in Sukie's possession, Queenie's documents and papers, Ephraim's secrecy, constant knitting and strict house rules). Let them reflect how, as readers, we are on the same journey as Olive, slowly piecing together the threads of the story. Discuss question 6 on the bookmark.

The Coastguard acts – a plan is revealed

Read at pace the next chapter, 'Freedom is in peril', pausing to consider how the incident with the spilled ink once again exacerbates the difficult relationship between Olive and Esther. As you read on through the passage describing Mr Spratt's meeting with the villagers, reflect on the feelings of distrust endemic in wartime, when people might be thrown together with strangers, and constantly warned to be aware of the risk of spies and enemy agents. Consider question 14 on the bookmark.

Tell the children that the camouflage of the lighthouse is based on historical fact: landmark buildings, including lighthouses, as well as ships, planes, tanks and guns were camouflaged by paint, or camouflage nets were draped over them to hide them from the enemy. Continue reading to the end of 'Keep it under your hat'. Ask the children what Olive has discovered about her sister, Sukie (that her pen pal was Ephraim, the lighthouse keeper).

Read on through 'Turning the tide' to the third chapter break. Encourage the children to note the asterisks indicating chapter breaks and consider what function they serve. (They mark a shift in time or location in the narrative). Link to question 7 on the bookmark. Ask a volunteer to summarise what Olive has learned about the secret plans and those involved. (It is a humanitarian mission to rescue Jewish people from German-occupied Europe; Ephraim, Queenie, Mrs Henderson, and Miss Carter are all involved.) Ask: *What remains unsolved?* (how Sukie might be involved) Read to the chapter end. Reflect how the children – as evacuees living without their parents or older sister – are learning to be brave and resourceful (Olive rescues Pixie, and Cliff, in turn, rescues her). At the chapter end, ask what the suitcase implies (that a boat carrying refugees is off the Devon coast – but may have got into trouble or even sunk).

A plane crashes – a boat arrives

Begin reading 'Hitler will send no warning'. Pause to ask what makes Olive cry (the thought that the boat carrying the refugees may have sunk, and that Sukie may have been on board with them). Point out that Olive has to use banana-flavoured parsnips for the sandwiches. Ask: *Can you suggest why bananas weren't available in the war?* (Ships importing foods from overseas were in danger of being attacked by enemy ships or submarines.) Refer back to question 11 on the bookmark. Read the episode describing the plane crash at pace then ask: *Why does Olive not want the lighthouse to be camouflaged?* (The boat carrying refugees has not arrived and might need guiding in to avoid the quicksand.) *When the plane crashes, why does she feel sympathy/empathy for the pilot?* (Her father has been killed in a plane crash in the war.)

Read on through the next two chapters, 'X marks the spot 'and 'Together', briefly discussing the idea of codes being important in the war for disguising information it was important to keep from enemy forces. Refer to question 3 on the bookmark. As Esther and Olive rescue the boat, reflect again on how the children are learning to become brave and resourceful without adults around them. At the chapter end, focus on the reunion between Esther and her father, and how this makes Olive feel.

Refugee stories – family news

Continue reading to the end of 'It's a full-time job to win'. Pause at the end of the chapter to ask what it is that Olive has realised (that Miss Carter was the person that Sukie met before she went missing). Read on through 'Coughs and sneezes spread diseases', pausing to note the shift in the relationship between Olive and Esther. Ask: *What has brought this about?* (They bonded when they rescued the refugee boat together.) Highlight that the quickest way for Olive to contact her mother when Cliff is ill is by telegram. Continue reading, pausing to ask what Olive has now discovered (that her mother was the London contact for the group, not Sukie). Raise questions 2 and 6 on the bookmark. Read the next chapter, 'Where skill and courage count', at pace. Ask: *How does Olive's mother justify not telling Olive the truth about Sukie's disappearance?* (She explains that in wartime, people have to think beyond family to the greater good, so as not to endanger more lives.) Tell the children that Esther's story about Kristallnacht is based on historical fact. Return to question 11 on the bookmark.

Together – in hope

As you read the next chapter, 'May you never know…', reflect how the villagers and refugees bond as they share food and music. At the end of the chapter, ask if they can guess what the stopped clocks in Queenie's house might represent. Continue reading the next chapter, 'Each little error…', asking a volunteer to explain how Olive and her mother encourage the other people at the party to protect Ephraim from arrest, and how they do it (by all claiming to share the guilt). Consider questions 4 and 14 on the bookmark.

Read 'V for victory' at pace. Pause at the chapter end to ask why Sukie missed the refugee boat. (She had met someone in France who had witnessed their father's plane crash and death.) Read on to the end of the novel. Ask: *How did their father's plane crash echo the German pilot's crash earlier in the story?* (They both deliberately avoided crashing into a building to try to save others' lives.) Ask: *How do you think Olive is feeling at the end of the story?* (hopeful) *Is it a happy and satisfactory ending to the story?* Encourage the children to give their reasons. Discuss question 12 on the bookmark.

Letters from the Lighthouse
By Emma Carroll

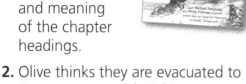

Focus on... Meaning

1. Explain the significance and meaning of the chapter headings.

2. Olive thinks they are evacuated to Devon to stay with Sukie's pen pal. What is the real reason?

3. What is the significance of the code Olive finds?

4. What does the author imply about the British government's policy towards Jewish refugees in World War II?

Focus on... Organisation

5. How do the chapter headings add content and interest?

6. How do Olive's gradual discoveries help shape the plot?

7. What function do the chapter breaks serve in organising the narrative?

Letters from the Lighthouse
By Emma Carroll

Focus on... Language and features

8. Identify words and phrases specific to the period and/or World War II.

9. How does the author use capital/ italic letters to convey or enhance meaning?

10. How does punctuation help convey meaning and/or structure the narrative?

Focus on... Purpose, viewpoint and effects

11. What does the novel tell us about how families' lives were affected in the war?

12. What do you think is the author's main message in the novel?

13. Who does Olive think would benefit from hearing Esther's tale and why?

14. Contrast the various attitudes shown by villagers towards strangers and refugees in the novel.

SHARED READING ▶

Extract 1

- Display and read Extract 1, from the first chapter. Underline the sentence 'She was running away from the shelter' and ask the children why this is puzzling to Olive. (An air raid is on, and everyone should be heading towards the shelter where they will be safe from the bombs.)

- Encourage the children to pick out words or terms associated with World War II. Circle the term 'air-raid warden' and ask the children if they can explain what his job was (to try to make sure everyone went into the safety of a shelter during an air raid). Circle or underline the acronym 'WRVS'. Can a volunteer recall what it stands for? (Women's Royal Voluntary Service)

- Focus on Olive's description of Sukie. Ask: *What was Sukie really doing? Which words that Olive uses about her sister are true?* ('she wouldn't think to keep herself safe')

- Circle or underline the words 'arms pumping like pistons' and ask a volunteer to explain the comparison. (Sukie's arms remind Olive of the mechanical parts driving a train.)

- Consider how the author creates drama and pace in this passage. Ask the children to pick out strong, active verbs ('sucked', 'smashed', 'fell', 'droned', 'swirled'). Ask: *What effect do they have?* (They suggest the sudden impact of the bomb.)

- Can they identify an onomatopoeic word which describes the sound of the bomb? ('*WHUMP*') Ask: *Why do you think the author uses both capital letters and italics?* (to emphasise how loud the sound is and how hard the bomb hits the ground) Highlight the use of ellipses. *What do they suggest?* (a tense pause before the bomb explodes)

Extract 2

- Read together Extract 2, from the chapter 'Hitler will send no warning'. Ask a volunteer to explain what is happening. (A German bomber plane has lost control and is heading for a crash landing.) Can they suggest what is wrong with the plane? (One of its engines is on fire.) Underline the phrase 'The truth was worse' and ask the children to explain what Olive most fears (that the plane will hit the lighthouse where Cliff and Pixie are).

- Ask: *Which words tell us how Olive is feeling?* ('I couldn't even scream: my heart was jammed in my throat.') *Why do you think she wants the other children to shut up?* (They are making it worse by excitedly saying the plane will hit the lighthouse.)

- Circle tricky vocabulary ('compelling', 'lurch', 'veered', 'bail') and ask volunteers to provide meaning and suggest replacements. Ask: *Why do you think it would be a compelling sight to watch?* (to see how and where the plane finally lands) Focus on words that describe the plane's erratic movements ('lurch', 'veered'). Ask: *What do they remind Olive of and why?* (someone drunk – 'almost drunkenly' – because it is lurching from side to side).

- Challenge the children to identify onomatopoeic words which describe the sounds the plane makes ('spluttering', 'splutter', 'shuddered').

- Highlight short and incomplete sentences ('Then silence. Another splutter. Silence.') Ask the children what impact they have. (They change the pace and enhance the drama.)

- Ask: *Can you recall why the German pilot does not bail out?* (He stays in the cockpit to try to steer the plane away from the lighthouse, as Cliff later tells his sister.)

Extract 3

- Display and read Extract 3 from the chapter 'Together'. Ask a volunteer to explain what the girls are trying to do (guide the refugee boat in safely). Ask: *Why is Esther in danger?* (She is running towards the beach where Olive knows there is dangerous quicksand.) Ask a volunteer to explain what quicksands are (liquid sand that can suck people or animals in). *What stops Esther hearing Olive's warning?* (the wind)

- Circle tricky words ('groyne', 'orientate') and ask volunteers to explain them.

- Challenge them to find a simile ('like wading through snowdrifts') and suggest what it implies.

- Ask: *How would you describe the mood of this passage in the novel?* (exciting, tense) *Which words tell us how Olive is feeling?* ('My heart leaped to my throat', 'I breathed out. Almost.') Ask children to pick out speech verbs ('called', 'yelled', 'cried', 'gasped'), noting how they help convey the sense of breathless panic.

- Circle the word 'bobbing' and identify it as a present participle: a verb form ending in '-ing' which comes after another verb ('was') and conveys continuous action. Challenge the children to identify other present participles ('dropping', 'rising', 'losing', 'coming', 'running', 'scrambling' and so on), considering how they add to the sense of dramatic, continuous action. Ask: *What effect does using them singly as incomplete sentences have?* (It suggests the erratic appearance of the light out at sea and increases the pace.)

- Focus on the punctuation. Ask: *What effect do the words in capital letters have?* (They suggest shouting.) Examine the use of exclamation marks and ask volunteers to suggest what impact they have. (They relay the excited, panicky voices of the girls.)

Extract 4

- Read Extract 4 together. Challenge the children to highlight a detail which is echoed in the novel. (The lighthouse was camouflaged.)

- Underline the sentence about the south-west coast and ask a volunteer to explain its meaning. (The British feared the Germans would invade.)

- Circle the term 'code-named' and ask a volunteer to explain the significance of codes in wartime, referring back to the novel. (They were used to hide information from the enemy.)

- Circle or underline tricky vocabulary ('impregnable', 'squat', 'disguised', 'dubbed', 'fortified', 'entanglements', 'extinguished', 'decoy', 'generate', 'masqueraded') and ask children to provide explanations and suggest replacements.

- Identify and circle war-related terminology ('pillboxes', 'forts', 'Luftwaffe', 'aerodromes', 'bombing raids') and again ask for explanations.

- Explore together the words that convey the idea of defence. ('impregnable', 'forts', 'defensive', 'guarded'). Identify and underline all the words and phrases which describe building or construction ('sprang up', 'dug', 'fortified', 'sprouted', 'constructed', 'cast', 'build', 'built'). Ask: *What do words like 'sprang' and 'sprouted' suggest?* (that they appeared suddenly)

- Can they explain the reference to 'Hadrian's Wall'? (The pillboxes were erected as a long line of defences – like the fortified wall the Romans built to defend the northern border of Roman Britain.)

- Focus on the idea of fake or trick defences and ask the children to identify all the words which describe them, circling them. ('fool', 'disguised', 'camouflage', 'dummy', 'decoy', 'masqueraded')

- Challenge the children to identify and list the key coastal defences mentioned in the text, briefly explaining the function of each. Tell them that we can still see today the remains of these wartime defences, including thousands of the gun emplacements called pillboxes.

Extract 1

'Sukie!' I yelled, waving madly. 'Over here!'

She was running away from the shelter. And fast too – faster than I'd ever seen her run before – her arms pumping like pistons. She didn't turn, or slow down. I don't think she even heard me.

The air-raid warden was yelling now. 'Bomb incoming! Get down!'

He threw himself on to the pavement. I wasn't quick enough. The telltale whistling came next… An eerie silence…

Then a *WHUMP* as the bomb hit just a few hundred yards away. The ground rocked underneath me. Air was sucked from my chest, making me gasp and stagger backwards, though somehow I stayed on my feet. Glass smashed, bricks fell, planes droned onwards. Everything swirled dizzily together. For a moment I didn't know which way the sky was.

As the dust cleared, my stunned brain did too. Twenty yards or so up ahead was my sister. She was limping slightly, with one of her shoes missing, but still rapidly disappearing down the street.

'Sukie!' I cried again in frustration. 'Wait! We're here!'

She was searching for us, I was certain, and knowing her, she wouldn't think to keep herself safe. She'd stay out here, not giving up until she found us. This was what terrified me. Cliff would be all right in the shelter with the WRVS lady. What mattered was getting hold of Sukie.

Side-stepping the air-raid warden as he got unsteadily to his feet, I ran after my sister. The warden shouted something, I didn't hear what.

'Sukie! Slow down!' I cried, gas-mask box bouncing at my hip.

She was too far ahead. A silly, random thought came to me of how nice her hair still looked as it swung against the green of Mum's coat. Then panic. I'd never catch up with her. I'd a stitch in my side and even hobbling with one shoe, she was still too quick for me.

Extract 2

It was obvious something was wrong with the plane. Thick black smoke trailed from the engine on the left. Flames were visible under the wing. There was another spluttering. Then silence. Another splutter. Silence. It was horrible yet compelling to watch.

About four hundred yards off the coast, the plane started losing height. It didn't drop down gently, either. There was a terrific lurch. The whole aircraft shuddered. It veered left, then right, almost drunkenly. I was afraid it was going to keep going and crash into the village. The truth was worse: it wouldn't make it that far.

Two hundred yards out to sea, the plane dropped further. The left wing dipped down. Straightened. The right one did the same. The horror of what was happening flashed before me: the German plane was on a collision course with the lighthouse. It'd never clear the top of the building. But it had to. Cliff and Pixie were still inside. Not that I could do anything, it was too late for that. I couldn't even scream: my heart was jammed in my throat.

'He's aiming right for it!' one of the Budmouth kids cried out.

'Flipping heck! He's going to hit it!'

'He must have a parachute. Why doesn't he bail out?'

I couldn't watch. Yet I couldn't bear not to. *Shut up*, I willed them all, hand pressed to my mouth, *just shut up*.

Extract 3

It was Esther who spotted it first. 'Light! Over to the left! Coming in fast!'

My heart leaped to my throat. There was the sound of scrabbling on the shingle as Esther rushed to the water's edge. In my torch beam, I glimpsed her knee-deep in the shallows.

'Can't see anything more!' she called. 'Whatever it was has gone!'

'False alarm.' I breathed out. Almost.

'Light!' Esther screamed gain. 'LIGHT! I said LIGHT!'

Sure enough, there in the blackness was a light. It was bobbing about wildly. Dropping. Rising. Dropping again. The sea was so huge we kept losing sight of it.

'They're coming in!' I yelled, straining on tiptoe. 'Over to the right – look!'

The light vanished again.

'They're heading for the rocks!' Esther cried.

'That's not rocks, that's the quicksands.'

She didn't hear me. She set off half running, half scrambling along the beach, heading straight towards the groyne.

I tried to shout: 'Wait! Don't go any further!' but the wind snatched my words away.

Wavering up ahead, I spotted the beam from Esther's torch. Thankfully, she wasn't that far away, though trying to run after her over the shingle was like wading through snowdrifts. Too quickly I grew exhausted. On my right was the sea, which helped orientate me. All the time the boat was coming closer. It was level with me now, and moving diagonally towards the shore.

'Esther, stop!' I yelled at the very top of my lungs. 'STOP!'

Her torch beam picked out the slimy black wood of the groyne. Just as she reached it, she slowed, looking over her shoulder to locate the boat; she was a little way ahead of it still. A blast of wind sent me stumbling forwards. In a few strides, I was able, at last, to reach her. I threw my arms around her waist and hung on tight.

'Don't go any further. It's quicksand!' I gasped.

Extract 4

Pillboxes and Tank Traps: coastal defences in World War II

By 1940, Nazi Germany, led by Adolf Hitler, was preparing to invade the British Isles. Hitler's plan was code-named 'Operation Sea Lion'. The south-west coast was considered a prime target.

In Britain, Winston Churchill's government launched a huge coastal defence programme designed to make the country an impregnable fortress. Thousands of concrete pillboxes sprang up along the coast. These small, squat forts were dug into the ground, then disguised with soil, grass and camouflage nets to provide safe cover for lookouts and guns. Each box was linked to the next by defensive ditches, dug deep enough to stop a tank in its tracks. One line, dubbed the 'Hadrian's Wall of the Twentieth Century', ran from Seaton in Devon all the way to Bridgwater in Somerset.

Natural defences such as shingle banks, rivers and canals were fortified with mines and barbed wire fencing. Coiled metal posts sprouted from the beaches, supporting entanglements of barbed wire. Cages of scaffolding tubes were constructed, and huge concrete blocks were cast on-site to prevent German tanks landing. Lighthouses were painted with camouflage paint and their lights often extinguished except to guide friendly craft ashore.

Tricks were also used to try to fool the Luftwaffe. Film studio designers and engineers were enlisted to build dummy aerodromes, factories and even whole towns, to act as decoy sites. Tanks of diesel, raised on towers, were burned then doused with water, to generate clouds of smoke and steam which masqueraded as successful bombing raids. Drainpipes were posted along the coastline to look like guns, dummy pillboxes were built, and uniformed shop dummies guarded the coast.

GRAMMAR, PUNCTUATION & SPELLING ▶

1. Not just nouns

Objective
To use expanded noun phrases to convey complicated information concisely.

What you need
Copies of *Letters from the Lighthouse*, enlarged copy of Extract 4, photocopiable page 22 'Not just nouns'.

What to do
- Display an enlarged copy of Extract 4 (Shared reading). Re-read the extract together, then circle or underline the words 'forts', 'posts' and 'blocks'. Ask the children if they can identify which part of speech they are (nouns). Examine the phrases which expand the nouns to describe them further: 'small, squat forts', 'Coiled metal posts', 'huge concrete blocks'.

- Tell the children we call this kind of phrase an 'expanded noun phrase'. It is a neat, concise way of telling us more about the subject (noun). Underline the adjectives which are the describing words in each phrase.

- Write a list of nouns on the board taken from the novel: for example, 'suitcase', 'coat', 'refugee', 'code'. Challenge children to think up noun phrases using one or more adjectives to describe them. (For example, 'heavy, waterlogged suitcase', 'warm, smart coat', 'tired, frightened refugee', 'hand-written secret code'.)

- Arrange the children into pairs and hand out photocopiable page 22 'Not just nouns'. Allow them time to fill in the sheet, then bring the class back together to review their noun phrases.

Differentiation
Support: As a class, create a list of adjectives to help children compose their phrases.

Extension: Let pairs choose more nouns from the novel and write noun phrases describing them.

2. Super subjunctives

Objective
To recognise vocabulary and structures that are appropriate for formal speech and writing, including subjunctive forms.

What you need
Copies of *Letters from the Lighthouse*.

What to do
- Tell the children that they are going to scan the novel and compile a list of formal orders that the British government might have issued during the war. This is an official document, so the language should be formal. They are going to practise using a verb form called the subjunctive, which can be used to express demands or orders in formal speech and writing. The verb can be present or past tense (they will be using the present) and active or passive. It is used in a subordinate clause linked to the main clause with 'that'.

- Write examples on the board, underlining the present subjunctive verb forms. For example, 'It is ordered that people <u>observe</u> the blackout; …the lighthouse keeper <u>log</u> all calls; …the lighthouse light <u>be extinguished</u>.' Point out that even in the third-person singular, the subjunctive ('log') keeps the same form, without an 's'.

- Ask pairs to search the novel for ideas of orders that might be issued (such as evacuating children from cities, using shelters during air raids, food rationing).

- Bring the class back together to share ideas before they begin drafting.

- When they have finished, invite volunteers to read aloud their orders, checking the subjunctive is used correctly.

Differentiation
Support: Provide a list of ideas for pairs to use for drafting their orders.

Extension: Let children use their own research to extend their list of orders.

3. Model modals

Objective

To use modal verbs or adverbs to indicate degrees of possibility.

What you need

Copies of *Letters from the Lighthouse*, photocopiable page 23 'Model modals'.

What to do

- Write on the board the sentence 'Olive thinks Sukie is a spy.' Ask the children if they think this statement is true. Discuss why Olive has her suspicions (because of clues she finds – like the code) but that she cannot be sure. Underline the verb 'is' in the sentence. Can they replace it with a verb that would suggest the possibility without making it a fact? For example, 'Olive thinks Sukie may be/could be/might be a spy.'

- Tell the children that verbs that indicate possibility are called modal verbs. Write on the board 'will', 'would', 'may', 'might', 'must', 'shall', 'should', 'can', 'could'. Point out that modal verbs are used to suggest something is possible but not certain, and they can even indicate how likely something is. Ask: *Which modal verb would make it sound very likely that Sukie is a spy?* ('must': 'Olive thinks Sukie must be a spy.')

- Tell the children that modal adverbs can be used for emphasis ('Olive thinks Sukie may possibly be a spy'; 'Olive thinks Sukie must definitely be a spy'.)

- Hand out photocopiable page 23 'Model modals' and let children complete it in pairs. Bring the class back together and share findings. In the first part, if children have chosen different modal verbs for the same sentence, which work best and why?

Differentiation

Support: Limit the task to choosing and writing verbs, then try adding adverbs as a shared activity.

Extension: Challenge pairs to compose more sentences using the same pattern.

4. Perfect perfects

Objective

To use the perfect forms of verbs to mark relationships of time and cause.

What you need

Copies of *Letters from the Lighthouse*.

What to do

- Begin by suggesting that after Sukie's disappearance, Olive has to take on a detective role to find out what happened to her. Often her suspicions are proven wrong as she gradually discovers the truth.

- Write on the board 'Olive thought Sukie was writing to Queenie. Who had she been writing to?' Encourage a volunteer to answer in a full sentence, writing it on the board and underlining the past-perfect verb forms in question and answer: 'Who <u>had</u> she <u>been writing</u> to? She <u>had been writing</u> to Ephraim.'

- Explain that the past-perfect verb form describes something that took place before the main narrative, shifting us back in time.

- Write some more statements and questions on the board, underlining the past-perfect verb: 'Olive thought Sukie was the secret contact. Who <u>had been</u> the secret contact?' Again, challenge a volunteer to answer in a full sentence, using the past-perfect verb: 'Mrs Bradshaw/Olive's mother <u>had been</u> the secret contact.'

- Arrange the children into pairs. Following the same pattern, let each write a statement and question about Olive's suspicions for their writing partner to answer using the past-perfect verb form.

- Bring the class back together to share ideas.

Differentiation

Support: Provide a list of statements and questions for pairs to answer.

Extension: Repeat the exercise using present and present-perfect verb tenses.

5. Verb swap

Objective

To use passive verbs to affect the presentation of information in a sentence.

What you need

Copies of *Letters from the Lighthouse*, copies of Extract 4.

What to do

- Re-read together Extract 4. Tell the children to focus on the verbs. Underline the verbs 'were dug', 'was linked', 'were fortified'. Identify these as passive verbs. Can the children pick out active verbs? ('sprang', 'sprouted').

- Focus on the passive forms and ask the children to replace them with active verbs ('They dug small, squat forts'; 'they linked them with defensive ditches' and so on). Ask why the passive may have been chosen here – because it is the defences that are the focus here, not the people who made them.

- Arrange the children into pairs and hand out copies of Extract 4. Challenge them to underline all the passive verbs in one colour. Let them repeat the exercise using another colour for all the active verbs. Challenge pairs to rewrite the passage using only active verbs. Remind them they will need to choose a subject for each active verb: for example, '<u>Hitler</u> code-named his plan…' or '<u>They/People/Teams</u> dug small, squat forts'.

- When they have finished, invite a volunteer to read aloud their text. Encourage challenges where passive verbs have not been changed to active. What effect does the use of only active verbs have? Point out how using both verb forms lends variety and avoids repeating subjects.

- Encourage children to look out for passive verbs in the novel and consider why the author may have chosen them.

Differentiation

Support: Let pairs choose two or three sentences from the text to work on.

Extension: Let pairs rewrite the passage using only passive verb forms.

6. Reliable relatives

Objective

To use relative clauses beginning with 'who', 'which', 'where', 'when', 'whose', 'that' or an implied (ie omitted relative pronoun).

What you need

Copies of *Letters from the Lighthouse*, photocopiable page 24 'Reliable relatives'.

What to do

- Write on the board a sentence from the novel, underlining the relative pronoun. (For example, 'On my right was the sea, <u>which</u> helped orientate me.')

- Tell the children that relative clauses can be used to identify or define a noun (in this case the noun 'the sea'). Explain that relative clauses are usually introduced by a relative pronoun, or the pronoun can be 'implied'. Demonstrate by writing another sentence from the novel: 'Emerging from an alleyway was a man I didn't recognise'. Ask: *What is the implied relative pronoun here?* (who/whom)

- List relative pronouns on the board ('who', 'which', 'where', 'when', 'whose', 'that'). Then write on the board the beginning of a sentence: 'Olive is an evacuee…'. Challenge volunteers to complete the sentence using different relative pronouns. For example, 'Olive is an evacuee who had to leave London during the war.' or 'Olive is an evacuee whose life changed when she left London.'

- Hand out photocopiable page 24 'Reliable relatives' and challenge pairs to complete it. Before they begin, read through the sentences together. Encourage the children to refer back to the novel to help them compose relative clauses that best complete each sentence.

- Bring the class back together and share work, encouraging constructive feedback on which sentences work best.

Differentiation

Support: Discuss and list facts about each subject to help children compose relative clauses.

Extension: Let children experiment using alternative relative pronouns in the sentences provided.

 # Not just nouns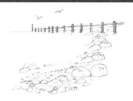

- Write an expanded noun phrase to describe each noun. Then use your phrase in a sentence about something that happened in the novel.

groyne

Expanded noun phrase: _____

Sentence: _____

_____

shingle

Expanded noun phrase: _____

Sentence: _____

_____

sea

Expanded noun phrase: _____

Sentence: _____

_____

cobbles

Expanded noun phrase: _____

Sentence: _____

_____

rocks

Expanded noun phrase: _____

Sentence: _____

_____

Model modals

- Choose a modal verb to fill the gap in each sentence. Try adding an adverb from the box or choose your own to emphasise the meaning.

modal verbs		
will	would	may
might	shall	should
can	could	must

adverbs		
probably	exactly	possibly
surely	obviously	easily
just	really	definitely

1. Olive thinks Sukie _____ be in the rescue boat.

2. Olive thinks they _____ help the German pilot.

3. Olive believes the villagers _____ learn from Esther's tale.

4. Olive thinks Cliff _____ fall off the ladder.

5. Olive thinks the German plane _____ hit the lighthouse.

6. Olive thinks Esther _____ fall into the quicksands.

7. Olive thinks Ephraim _____ like Sukie when he meets her.

Now try writing two sentences of your own about something from the book, use the model verbs and adverbs above.

1. _____

_____

2. _____

_____

Reliable relatives

- Complete the relative clauses to fill the gap in each sentence. Refer back to the novel to help you find facts you can use.

1. The day when _____ was a Friday in January.

2. Olive, who _____, thinks they will be staying with Sukie's penpal.

3. Esther, whose _____, helped rescue the boat.

4. The code, that _____, showed plans for landing on the Devon coast.

5. Queenie, whose _____, set all her clocks at 2.10.

6. The lighthouse, which _____, had to be camouflaged.

7. The land, where _____, belonged to the Wilcoxes.

- Write your own sentence about a character or topic from the novel, using a relative pronoun.

_____

_____

_____

PLOT, CHARACTER & SETTING ▶

1. Key events

> ### Objective
> To identify how language, structure and presentation contribute to meaning.
>
> ### What you need
> Copies of *Letters from the Lighthouse*; scissors; glue; photocopiable page 29 'Key events'.

What to do

- Challenge children to summarise the main narrative of the novel. Encourage them to suggest one event in the novel which is crucial to the plot and one event which is dramatic or exciting but which does not drive the plot. (For example, the rescue of the refugee boat is crucial to the plot; the crash of the German plane is dramatic, but not crucial to the plot.)

- Arrange the children into pairs and hand out photocopiable page 29 'Key events'. Explain that they need briefly to describe how each event drives the plot then cut and paste them in the order in which they happen.

- When they have finished, bring the class back together. Suggest that these are the key events which help to structure the novel.

- Challenge volunteers to cite examples of events which make the plot more interesting or exciting, but which do *not* drive the main narrative (for example, Olive having a fight with Esther or Pixie falling into the quicksand). Encourage the children to back up their suggestions with reasons. Reflect how, although these events do not directly drive the plot, they contribute to the way the author builds character and setting.

> ### Differentiation
> **Support:** Explore the images together, checking that the children can interpret the events.
>
> **Extension:** Challenge pairs to add more events to the sequence.

2. Britain at war

> ### Objective
> To summarise the main ideas drawn from more than one paragraph, identifying key details that support the main ideas.
>
> ### What you need
> Copies of *Letters from the Lighthouse*.
>
> ### Cross-curricular link
> History

What to do

- Tell the children they are going to focus on the novel's wartime setting. Invite them to come up with key facts about the period and locations of the novel, noting them on the board (1941/2; London and the Devon coast).

- Challenge them to cite some of the ways the war affected life in Britain in the early 1940s which we can learn from the novel. List ideas on the board such as 'bombing raids (the Blitz)'; 'men away fighting'; 'home defences/safety precautions'; 'child evacuees'; 'food shortages'.

- Ask pairs to use the headings listed on the board to skim and scan the novel for information about life during the war, and to note their findings.

- When they have finished, bring the class back together to share findings. Encourage children to volunteer other information they may know about the war from family history and experiences.

- Ask children to choose one of the headings and to develop their notes into a paragraph, with illustrations.

> ### Differentiation
> **Support:** Briefly discuss each topic before children begin work, referring to relevant detail from the novel.
>
> **Extension:** Let children use their own research from books, the internet or their family history to add detail.

3. The Bradshaws

Objective
To identify how language, structure and presentation contribute to meaning.

What you need
Copies of *Letters from the Lighthouse*, photocopiable page 30 'The Bradshaws'.

Cross-curricular links
History, PSHE

What to do

- Tell the children they are going to focus on Olive's family. Together, list the facts we know about the Bradshaw family: names, ages, school, work. Ask the children to suggest some ways their everyday family life has been affected by the war (their mother is tired, sad and working too hard; their father is missing in action, presumed dead; the children's school is closed, and they have to be evacuated from London).

- Suggest that because of events that happen in the novel, Olive learns lots of things about the members of her family which she did not know before.

- Provide pairs with photocopiable page 30 'The Bradshaws'. Explain that they should write down what Olive knows about each family member at the start of the novel, and what she has discovered about them by the end. They should refer back to the novel to help them find information. For example, Olive knows her mother is sad because she has been widowed; she works at the printing works; she needs rest because she is tired and unwell. By the end of the novel, she has discovered that she does secret and brave humanitarian war work.

- Bring the class back together to share findings. Reflect on how the war changes not just everyday life, but also how Olive views her family.

Differentiation
Support: Before pairs begin, briefly discuss each character, citing relevant parts of the novel.

Extension: Encourage pairs to consider what Olive discovers about herself, adding notes to their sheet.

4. Sukie

Objective
To draw inferences such as inferring characters' feelings, thoughts and motives from their actions, and to justify inferences with evidence.

What you need
Copies of *Letters from the Lighthouse*.

Cross-curricular link
PSHE

What to do

- Suggest that Sukie is arguably the most important character in the plot. Ask: *Can you suggest why?* (She is the one who goes missing; she is given the code; she goes to Europe to help save people; she appears at the end of the story.)

- Begin by asking a volunteer to summarise Sukie's actions. (She takes her mother's place and goes to Europe to help rescue the refugees.) Ask: *Can you explain her motives?* (She is upset by what is happening to the Jewish people and wants to help them; she is also concerned about her mother and wants her to rest.)

- Together, list words and phrases to describe Sukie. Encourage the children to consider both her strengths and weaknesses: she is independent, selfless and brave but she can also be reckless, naïve and impulsive.

- Write on the board the headings 'Appearance', 'Action' and 'Dialogue'. Arrange the children into pairs and challenge them to skim and scan the novel for examples from each category that convey Sukie's character.

- Challenge children to work individually to write a short character profile of Sukie, explaining how she is crucial to the plot of the novel.

Differentiation
Support: Write on the board one example under each heading to get children started.

Extension: Challenge children to write an episode from the novel from Sukie's point of view.

5. Predictions

Objectives
To predict what might happen from details stated and implied; to identify how language, structure and presentation contribute to meaning.

What you need
Copies of *Letters from the Lighthouse*, photocopiable page 31 'Predictions'.

What to do

- Briefly discuss the genre of the novel (wartime, mystery). Ask: *What is the mystery that Olive has to solve?* (Why Sukie vanished and what has happened to her.) Discuss how Olive uses detective skills to unravel the mystery. Along the way, she discovers clues that she has to piece together and, as readers, we follow the trail with her.

- Suggest that sometimes the author plants clues which we may realise before Olive does. Explain that the children are going to explore the way these clues encourage us to read on to find out what happens next.

- Arrange the class into pairs and hand out photocopiable page 31 'Predictions'. Allow the children time to complete it, skimming and scanning the novel to find relevant information.

- Bring the class back together and share findings. Discuss how the mystery, which is set up in the first chapter, is solved in stages as the plot unfolds. Encourage the children to consider how this is one way the author structures the plot. As readers we are encouraged to question Olive's beliefs and guess at the truth: for example, Olive believes Queenie is Sukie's pen pal, but why does Queenie never want to talk about her?

Differentiation
Support: Direct children to relevant chapters to find information.

6. Destination: Devon

Objective
To ask questions to improve their understanding.

What you need
Copies of *Letters from the Lighthouse*; a map of the UK; railway timetables (optional).

Cross-curricular links
Geography, mathematics

What to do

- Briefly recap why Olive and Cliff are evacuated (to escape the bombing in London). Explain that Budmouth Point, where they are evacuated to, is a fictional place based on Start Point in south Devon. Together, look at a map of the UK, focusing on the distance between London and Start Point. Discuss how long the journey might take now by car or train (roughly 220 miles, or 354km – over 5 hours). Then remind the children that steam trains were used in the 1940s, so the journey would have taken much longer. Refer back to the novel for clues ('It was dark when we finally arrived').

- Set up a role play activity to compare and contrast the children's lives in Devon and London. Let volunteers take the roles of Olive and Cliff. Groups should prepare questions to ask them about their lives in Devon compared to London, such as: *What do you enjoy in Devon?* (the sea and beach, the fresh air, the lighthouse) *What do you miss about London?* (the cinema, their school, family and friends) Let volunteers from each group ask their questions and encourage children to speculate and give feedback on the answers.

Differentiation
Support: List information on the two locations on the board for children to refer to.

Extension: Let children use the internet to read stories by children evacuated to Devon (for example, BBC WWII People's War).

7. Esther Wirth

Objective
To draw inferences such as inferring characters' feelings, thoughts and motives from their actions, and to justify inferences with evidence.

What you need
Copies of *Letters from the Lighthouse*.

Cross-curricular links
PSHE, RE

What to do

- Tell the children to focus on the character of Esther. Ask: *How does Olive first meet Esther and what are her first impressions?* (Esther snatches Cliff's comic; she seems rude and unfriendly.)

- Let children work in small groups to skim and scan the novel for information about Esther. They should make notes about her family; where she lived; what happened to her family and how she came to be in Devon.

- Bring the class together to discuss how and why Olive's opinion of Esther changes during the novel, prompting them with questions on the board: *What does Olive learn about Esther's past?* (She has lost her mother, brother and family dog, and she has been uprooted from her home and everything she knows.) *How does Olive help Esther?* (She helps rescue the boat with her father on board.) *How does Esther's father help Olive's family?* (He is a doctor and diagnoses Cliff's illness.) *How does Esther help to make the village a better and more understanding place?* (She helps them understand the plight of the Jewish refugees fleeing Nazi Germany.) Encourage the children to consider what they think the author's message is concerning refugees.

- Challenge children to work individually to draft Esther's records/documents for the Kindertransport, recording key facts about her family and history.

Differentiation
Support: Support children in finding relevant information.

Extension: Let children do their own research to find out more about the Kindertransport.

8. Big events

Objective
To understand what they read by summarising the main ideas drawn from more than one paragraph, identifying key details that support the main ideas.

What you need
Copies of *Letters from the Lighthouse*.

Cross-curricular link
History

What to do

- Tell the children they are going to focus on the way the author uses dramatic events to help structure the narrative.

- Begin by arranging them into small groups. Assign each group three or four chapters (there are 25 altogether). Challenge them to note down all the 'big events' that happen in each of their chapters. When they have finished, bring the class back together and invite groups – in random order of chapter coverage – to cite the key events, listing them on the board. (For example: 'Keep calm and carry on' – air raid; 'Together' – Olive and Esther rescue refugee boat.)

- Challenge groups to rearrange the events listed on the board in the order they happen in the plot. When they have finished, they should discuss in their groups whether those events are directly caused by the war – for example, the air raid is caused by the war, but Cliff becoming ill is not.

- Bring the class back together to share their ideas. Encourage children to discuss and compare the story with other novels or films about WWII evacuees they are familiar with (*Carrie's War, Goodnight Mister Tom*) focusing on the main characters, and how the wartime setting fosters dramatic events and changes in their lives.

Differentiation
Support: List findings in chronological order, discussing as a class what causes each event.

Extension: Repeat the exercise for the other novels with wartime settings.

Key events

- Write a sentence describing how each of the following events drive the plot of the novel. Then cut out the boxes and place them in the order they happen.

The Bradshaws

- Write some facts Olive knows about her family at the start of the novel, and something new she has discovered about them by the end of the novel.

	What Olive knows at the start	What Olive discovers later
Mrs Bradshaw		
Mr Bradshaw		
Sukie		
Cliff		

Predictions

- Write down the truth behind Olive's beliefs and explain how she finds it out.

What Olive believes	What really happened?	When/how does Olive find out the truth?
Olive believes Sukie was meeting her boyfriend.		
Olive believes her mother was killed in the air raid.		
Olive believes Queenie was Sukie's pen pal.		
Olive believes the refugee boat must have sunk.		

TALK ABOUT IT ▶

1. Evacuees growing up

Objective
To maintain attention and participate actively in collaborative conversations, staying on topic and initiating and responding to comments.

What you need
Copies of *Letters from the Lighthouse*, photocopiable page 35 'Evacuees growing up'.

Cross-curricular links
History, PSHE

What to do
- Remind the children that in the first chapter, Sukie takes Olive and Cliff to the cinema before she vanishes. Discuss how Olive feels when she realises they are alone (anxious, nervous, unsure). Ask: *What tells us that Olive usually relies on Sukie as her elder sister?* (Her first thought is finding Sukie; then she realises she must be the big/responsible sister; she tries to reassure Cliff but is really scared and unsure; she is relieved when an adult takes charge.) *Do you think Olive has changed by the end of the story and if so how?* Encourage children to express opinions. (She has to learn to manage alone, without Mum or Sukie; she becomes more confident and mature and understands more.)

- Ask pairs to complete photocopiable page 35 'Evacuees growing up'. Prompt them to discuss how a child might feel in each situation and then how Olive behaves. Ask: *Does she seem grown up/mature?*

- Bring the class back together and use their answers to begin a discussion on how, as an evacuee, Olive grows in maturity and confidence.

Differentiation
Support: Read the photocopiable sheet together as a class, referring back to relevant text before they begin.

2. Careless talk costs lives

Objective
To use spoken language to develop understanding through speculating, hypothesising, imagining and exploring ideas.

What you need
Copies of *Letters from the Lighthouse*.

Cross-curricular link
History

What to do
- Write on the board 'Careless talk costs lives', 'Walls have ears', 'Loose lips sink ships'. Remind the children that these chapter titles were all slogans of government campaigns during World War II. Ask volunteers to explain what they mean. Suggest that keeping secrets is an important theme in the novel. Ask: *Why would keeping secrets be so important in wartime?* (to avoid important information falling into enemy hands)

- Arrange the children into pairs and write three headings on the board: 'Name/s', 'Secret', 'Reasons'. Challenge the children to think of all the people in the novel who keep secrets. They should divide their writing paper into three columns using the headings, then write down the names of characters who keep secrets, what the secret is, and what their reasons are for keeping that secret, discussing their ideas together. Model one example: 'Sukie', 'takes her mother's place to meet Queenie', 'wants her mother to rest'.

- Allow them time to complete the task, referring back to the novel to help them. When they have finished, bring the class back together. Ask volunteers to share ideas. Encourage children to discuss each secret, deciding if they think it was justified and, if so, why.

Differentiation
Support: Provide a list of characters who keep secrets (Sukie, Mrs Bradshaw, Queenie, Ephraim, Miss Carter).

Extension: Encourage children to explore the same theme in other novels set in the war.

3. Changing minds

Objective
To use spoken language to develop understanding through speculating, hypothesising, imagining and exploring ideas.

What you need
Copies of *Letters from the Lighthouse*.

Cross-curricular links
History, PSHE

What to do

- Tell the children they are going to think about the way the people at Budmouth Point behave towards the refugees who come to live in their community. Discuss words to describe their different reactions ('hostile', 'suspicious', 'resentful', 'welcoming', 'friendly', 'warm')

- Challenge the children to recall attempts that are made to change minds and make the community more welcoming and accepting. List ideas on the board: Mr Barrowman's talk to the school children; Esther's sewing idea; Esther's idea for a tea party.

- Discuss which attempts are most effective and why. Ask: *How do the children react to Mr Barrowman's talk and why? What does Esther's idea achieve which just talking to the children doesn't?* (She makes the children empathise with the refugees as individuals.) *What does the tea party achieve?* (It makes the refugees feel welcome, and everyone comes together through their shared enjoyment of food and dancing.)

- Arrange the children into small groups. Encourage them to think of ideas of how to make refugees or newcomers feel welcome in their own community. Bring the class back together to share ideas and invite constructive feedback.

Differentiation
Support: List the attempts/initiatives on the board for children to discuss.

Extension: Choose the best group ideas and allow time for children to develop them as plans for community initiatives or events.

4. War words

Objective
To use relevant strategies to build their vocabulary.

What you need
Copies of *Letters from the Lighthouse*, photocopiable page 36 'War words'.

Cross-curricular link
History

What to do

- Tell the children they are going to explain and use some of the words and terms in the novel which are specific to the wartime period in which the story is set.

- Hand out photocopiable page 36 'War words'. Invite volunteers to suggest meanings for each of the words and terms listed. They can refer back to the novel to help them. Encourage children to think which words are specific to the war, and which to the period (1940s). Encourage constructive feedback.

- Ask pairs to complete the photocopiable sheet. Explain that they should discuss the meaning of each word or term before using it in a sentence related to the novel, which clearly brings out its meaning. Demonstrate this by focusing on the term 'Picture Palace' (cinema) and writing on the board: 'Sukie takes Olive and Cliff to the Picture Palace to see *The Mark of Zorro.*'

- Bring the class back together and invite volunteers to read aloud their sentences. Compare sentences using the same word or term and invite children to reflect which sentences bring out the meaning most clearly.

- If there is time, challenge pairs to perform a role play activity featuring Olive and the air raid warden, using as many of the terms as they can.

Differentiation
Support: Provide meanings for each of the words and challenge pairs to use them in sentences.

Extension: Let children find other words or terms relating to the war from the novel to create a glossary.

5. Missing in action

Objective
To participate in discussions.

What you need
Copies of *Letters from the Lighthouse*; images of the Tomb of the Unknown Warrior, Westminster; The Cenotaph, Whitehall and of war graves in northern France.

Cross-curricular links
History, PSHE

What to do
- Challenge volunteers to identify images of the Tomb (for an unidentified soldier killed in the First World War) and the Cenotaph (a memorial for all those killed fighting for their country). Ask if the children know the days when soldiers are remembered each year (Remembrance Sunday and 11th November). Discuss as a class their significance: to remember and honour dead soldiers. Display the image of the war graves and invite children to consider the importance of maintaining war cemeteries, discussing why people want to visit and pay their respects.

- Focus on the moment when Sukie explains how her father died and where he is buried. Speculate how Olive feels hearing this news – why might hearing it be upsetting yet healing? What does Sukie suggest to her mother? (*They can go and visit the place where her father is buried.*)
Challenge the children to write a paragraph from Olive's point of view, describing a visit they subsequently make, and how it makes them feel. If they prefer, they can write in Rachel or Cliff's voice.

Differentiation
Support: Provide information about the images and direct the children to the passage about Monsieur Bonet.

Extension: Encourage children to suggest ways of supporting families who have lost loved ones in war.

6. War work

Objective
To give well-structured descriptions; to participate in presentations.

What you need
Copies of *Letters from the Lighthouse*, internet access, photocopiable page 37 'War work'.

Cross-curricular link
History

What to do
- Tell the children they are going to focus on jobs on the 'home front' (in Britain) during the war. Challenge the children to list jobs that are mentioned in the novel (air-raid wardens, coastguard, WRVS, railway workers, farmers, schoolteachers).

- Explain that some jobs on the home front were 'reserved occupations' which exempted people from joining up to fight in the war. Can they suggest jobs that might be essential to keep filled at home? (teachers, doctors, farmers, railway workers, utility workers) Tell them that others who were not called up to fight could volunteer for war work. People volunteered to be air-raid wardens, fire watchers, munitions workers (working in weapons factories) and Home Guard (protecting Britain from German invasion).

- Arrange the children into pairs. Hand out photocopiable page 37 'War work'. Encourage them to scan the novel for references to the jobs. Provide access to the internet and tell them to research each job. They can consider uniform, responsibilities, type of work and so on. They should make notes on their findings for a short presentation.

- Bring the class together and invite volunteers to deliver their presentation. They should try to describe clearly and concisely what each job involved. Encourage other children to contribute information.

Differentiation
Support: Direct children to relevant websites to find information.

Extension: Encourage pairs to research other jobs listed on the board.

Evacuees growing up

- Explain how Olive shows us she is growing in confidence and maturity in each situation.

When she sends postcards home to her mother.

_____
_____
_____
_____
_____
_____

When she first arrives at Queenie's house.

_____
_____
_____
_____
_____
_____

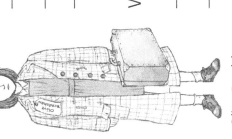

Olive Bradshaw

When she realises the refugee boat is due.

_____
_____
_____
_____
_____
_____

When Cliff is in danger or ill.

_____
_____
_____
_____
_____
_____

When the German pilot crashes his plane.

_____
_____
_____
_____

War words

- Discuss the meaning of each word or term. Then write a sentence relating to the novel which clearly brings out its meaning.

Air raid: _____

_____

_____

Gas mask: _____

_____

_____

Luftwaffe: _____

_____

Telegram: _____

_____

_____

_____

Picture Palace: _____

_____

Evacuee: _____

_____

War work

- Explain how each job features in the novel then use your own research to write down some facts about each job.

Job	In the novel	Facts from my research
WRVS		
Air-raid warden		
Coastguard		

GET WRITING ▶

1. Mother's news

Objective
To identify the audience for and purpose of the writing, selecting the appropriate form and using other similar writing as models for their own.

What you need
Copies of *Letters from the Lighthouse*, examples of playscripts.

Cross-curricular link
Drama

What to do
- Tell the children they are going to draft the script for a play scene, in which Rachel Bradshaw tells Olive and Cliff they are going to be evacuated. Re-read together 'Mothers: send them out of London', from 'It was then I properly took notice of the suitcases on the table' as far as 'The noise hit us the moment we left the bus'.

- Explain that they should extract and edit relevant dialogue from this passage, and add their own. Write the names of key characters on the board (Mrs Bradshaw, Gloria, Olive, Cliff).

- Arrange the children into groups of four. They should note down key points: what Mrs Bradshaw and Gloria tell the children (where they are going and why) and how the children react (nervous and worried at first, but excited at the idea of seeing the sea and lighthouse).

- Show examples of playscripts to familiarise them with how to set out dialogue. Allow them time to draft their scene, then bring the class back together and invite groups to perform their script for the class.

Differentiation
Support: Model a few lines of dialogue on the board to get them started.

Extension: Ask groups to perform their scenes, using tone and expression to convey feeling and emotion.

2. Olive's diary

Objective
To plan their writing by considering how authors have developed characters and settings in what pupils have read.

What you need
Copies of *Letters from the Lighthouse*.

What to do
- Remind the children of the postcards that Olive writes home to her mother: one when the children first arrive at Queenie's; the second after the German pilot crashes his plane. Invite volunteers to read them aloud. Re-visit why Olive doesn't write the truth to her mother (she wants to save her more worry). Tell them they are going to write entries for Olive's diary which would be truthful about these events and record her real feelings.

- Arrange the children into pairs and let each choose which postcard to rewrite. Before they begin, they should re-read the chapters in which the postcards feature: 'Do your duty' and 'X marks the spot'. Remind them that they should skim and scan the narrative, summarising key events before they begin, and also make notes on how Olive is feeling.

- Allow them time to draft their diary entries. Then let them repeat the exercise for the other postcard, before comparing their drafts with their writing partner's. Encourage children to share constructive criticism and edit their diary entries to improve them.

Differentiation
Support: Scan chapters as a shared activity, noting key points on the board.

Extension: Let children draft another entry for Olive's diary on a day they choose from the story.

3. Super similes

Objective

To discuss and evaluate how authors use language, including figurative language, considering the impact on the reader.

What you need

Copies of *Letters from the Lighthouse*, photocopiable page 41 'Super similes'.

What to do

- Tell the children that they are going to focus on the author's language and, in particular, her use of similes. Display Extracts 1 and 3 and ask them to find examples of similes ('her arms pumping like pistons'; 'trying to run… was like wading through snowdrifts'). Underline them.

- Encourage the children to consider how the comparisons help enhance the image in the reader's mind. Note that the first simile describes a visual image; the second suggests what it feels like.

- Provide writing materials and challenge the children to write a pair of sentences containing similes that describe a) the look of the quicksand on the beach by the lighthouse and b) the feel of it.

- Hand out photocopiable page 41 'Super similes' and let children work in pairs to complete it.

- When they have finished, bring the class back together to review their work. Invite volunteers to read aloud the sentences they have rewritten, encouraging constructive feedback. Which phrases do the children find most effective and why?

Differentiation

Support: Discuss the sentences as a class before they rewrite them, and help generate ideas for similes.

Extension: Challenge pairs to write more sentences containing similes describing characters or places in the novel.

4. Night-time rescue

Objective

To summarise the main ideas drawn from more than one paragraph.

What you need

Copies of *Letters from the Lighthouse*, photocopiable page 42 'Night-time rescue'.

Cross-curricular link

Art and design

What to do

- Re-read the chapter 'Together' from 'Down on the beach, there was no sign of Queenie…' to the end of the chapter.

- Tell the children to imagine they are preparing to film the scene for a movie. Explain that filmmakers often make storyboards before filming – a sequence of pictures showing how the action develops. Write on the board the headings 'Characters', 'Setting' and 'Action'. Tell them that each scene in a storyboard should record who appears, where the scene is set and what is happening.

- Arrange the children into pairs and provide photocopiable page 42 'Night-time rescue'. Tell them to skim and scan the passage and decide on six scenes to illustrate. Encourage them to make notes for each scene and include detail such as sound effects (the waves crashing, feet crunching through the shingle, a baby crying) and panoramic or close-up camera shots.

- Bring the class back together and write the best suggestions on the board. Encourage feedback. Ask: *Where could a panoramic shot work well?* (The bobbing light in a stormy sea?) *Where might a close-up shot be effective?* (Esther's face when she recognises her father?)

- Let the children, in their pairs, sketch the six storyboard scenes they have briefed using the other side of the photocopiable sheet.

Differentiation

Support: Provide support in choosing scenes and model notes for one scene on the board.

Extension: Let the children choose another episode to storyboard.

5. Poetic lighthouses

Objectives
To draft and write by selecting appropriate grammar and vocabulary, understanding how such choices can change and enhance meaning; to perform their own compositions, using appropriate intonation and volume.

What you need
Copies of *Letters from the Lighthouse*, images of lighthouses by day and night, photocopiable page 43 'Poetic lighthouses'.

Cross-curricular links
Geography, history

What to do
- Discuss all the ways the lighthouse features in the novel: Olive and Cliff are excited to see it, live with the lighthouse keeper, a German plane nearly crashes into it and so on. Ask: *What does the lighthouse represent to the people of Budmouth Point?* Remind the children that the author is fascinated by lighthouses as they represent 'a beacon of hope' – a main theme of the novel.

- Tell the children they are going to write a poem about a lighthouse. Show them images of lighthouses and discuss their function, where you see them, how they work and so on. Ask children to describe lighthouses they have seen or visited.

- Hand out photocopiable page 43 'Poetic lighthouses' to individuals or pairs. Tell them they should use the page to plan a short poem about a lighthouse. Share ideas on potential themes for the poem, for example, seeing the lighthouse for the first time or a camouflaged lighthouse. It may also benefit the children to discuss ideas on who or what speaks the words of their poem, for example a ship approaching the lighthouse or perhaps the lighthouse itself? Allow children time to fill in the plans then draft a short poem.

- Let children prepare a performance of their poem for the class, using intonation, volume and expression to enhance meaning.

Differentiation
Extension: Challenge children to use a range of poetic devices, for example similes, metaphors, personification, onomatopoeia, alliteration and repetition).

6. Esther's brilliant idea

Objective
To use organisational and presentational devices to structure text and guide the reader such as headings, bullet points, underlining.

What you need
Copies of *Letters from the Lighthouse*.

Cross-curricular link
PSHE

What to do
- Ask the children to recall Esther's idea for bringing locals and refugees together and what inspired it. (She is inspired, by sharing sandwiches with Olive, to plan a party.)

- Tell them to imagine they are going to draw up plans for the party. Arrange the children into pairs. They should first read the chapter 'May you never know what it means to be a refugee' from 'Esther's idea was to hold a tea party' (third chapter break), to the end of the following chapter. They should scan the text and note down all the preparations that Esther and Olive make for the party. Encourage them to consider things they will need (invitations, food, plates, tables?) and tasks that need to be done by the children, from delivering invitations to making cakes, sandwiches and so on.

- When they have made notes, they should consider how to structure their notes into a concise and organised plan, using bullet points or numbered instructions, for example.

- Allow the children time to scan the chapters and draw up their plans, then invite pairs to present them to the class, encouraging others to contribute to ideas.

Differentiation
Support: As a class, discuss and list headings for plans (invitations, food, music and so on) using organisational and presentational devices.

Extension: Let children work in pairs or small groups to plan their own party to welcome refugees or newcomers to their community.

 # Super similes

- Underline the simile in each sentence, then explain how the comparison helps us to imagine the scene. The first one has been done for you.

1. Luftwaffe bombs were falling on London like pennies falling from a jar.

_____

_____

2. The wind blew me like a leaf up the hill.

_____

_____

3. The man was dressed in black oilskins that made him look like a whale.

_____

_____

- Rewrite the following sentences to include a simile to help enhance the image.

1. Just beyond the harbour was a blackened hedge.

_____

_____

2. Thick carrot soup was ladled into bowls.

_____

_____

3. The sand covered her shoulders and was creeping up her neck.

_____

_____

Night-time rescue

- Use this page to plan scenes for a film of Olive and Esther rescuing the refugee boat.

Character/s:	Character/s:
Setting:	Setting:
Action:	Action:

Character/s:	Character/s:
Setting:	Setting:
Action:	Action:

Poetic lighthouses

- Use these questions and ideas to help you plan a lighthouse poem.

What is the theme of your poem?

_____

_____

_____

Who or what speaks the words of your poem?

_____

_____

_____

What happens in your poem?

_____

_____

_____

_____

List some words or phrases describing your lighthouse.

_____

_____

_____

_____

Write a simile or metaphor about a lighthouse that you will use in your poem.

_____

_____

_____

ASSESSMENT ▶

1. Useful relatives

Objective
To use relative clauses to join sentences.

What you need
Copies of *Letters from the Lighthouse*, flash cards with names of characters or subjects from novel.

What to do
- Arrange the class into pairs. Hand each pair a flash card with a name of a character or subject from the novel (Olive, Sukie, Cliff, Queenie, Ephraim, the lighthouse, Budmouth Point).

- Tell each pair to write down two short, factual sentences about their subject. They can refer to the novel to help them. Model one pair on the board: 'Queenie lived at the Post Office.' and 'Queenie took Olive and Cliff into her home.' Point out how the relative pronoun 'her', in the second sentence, avoids repeating the subject.

- When they have drafted sentences, list relative pronouns on the board ('who', 'which', 'where', 'when', 'whose', 'that'). Challenge children to join their sentences using a relative pronoun. Demonstrate on the board by writing 'Queenie, who lived at the Post Office, took Olive and Cliff into her home.'

- Repeat the exercise, asking pairs to swap their flash cards to work on another name or subject.

- When they have finished, invite pairs to read their sentences aloud. Ask: *Which relative pronouns have been used? Are there any that have not been used?* If so, encourage pairs to choose one of the names or subjects and compose a sentence aloud, using that pronoun.

Differentiation
Support: As a class, draft pairs of short sentences then ask pairs to try joining them.

Extension: Challenge pairs to use all the listed pronouns.

2. War themes

Objective
To summarise the main ideas drawn from more than one paragraph.

What you need
Copies of *Letters from the Lighthouse*.

Cross-curricular link
PSHE

What to do
- Ask the children to identify the main themes in the novel. (For example, finding hope in dark times; the lighthouse as a beacon of hope; learning compassion for refugees.) Write ideas on the board, prompting them with questions as necessary. Ask: *What does the lighthouse represent in the novel? What is the author's message about refugees in wartime?* Encourage children to identify devices the author uses to convey the themes. (For example, the lighthouse is a symbol of light/hope in darkness; Esther's story is a way of conveying the plight of refugees.)

- If the class or individuals have read any novels that cover similar themes (for example, World War II, child evacuees), invite comparisons, encouraging subjective opinion about plot, style, characters and setting.

- Ask children to choose the theme they think is most significant, or which had the most impact on them. They should draft a short paragraph beginning 'I think *Letters from the Lighthouse* is a novel about…' describing the theme and why they think it is important.

- Invite volunteers to read out their paragraphs, encouraging constructive feedback.

Differentiation
Support: Provide a list of key themes then let them choose the one they think is most significant and draft notes.

Extension: Children can construct mind maps showing key themes in the novel with notes about each.

3. Key characters

Objective
To give well-structured descriptions, explanations and narratives for different purposes, including for expressing feelings.

What you need
Copies of *Letters from the Lighthouse*, flash cards with names of key characters (Olive, Sukie, Mrs Bradshaw, Queenie, Ephraim, Esther).

What to do
- Tell the children they are going to try to summarise how key characters are important to the plot in as few words as possible. Explain that you will hold up flash cards with characters' names, and volunteers should then summarise, in under 30 seconds, how they are important to the plot. They should follow the same sentence pattern saying, for example, 'Olive is important to the plot because…'.

- Begin with Olive. Ask for a volunteer to summarise why she is important to the plot, using the stopwatch. (She is the narrator, who tells the story; she is determined to crack the code and find out what happened to Sukie.) Encourage children to suggest why the author chose a character to tell the story in the first person. (It gives a more personal slant as we see things through Olive's eyes.)

- Repeat the challenge for the other key characters, asking for volunteers to summarise why each character is important to the plot. Encourage others to give constructive feedback and add ideas.

Differentiation
Support: Let children make notes for each character before attempting spoken answers.

Extension: Let children follow up answers by discussing more widely what each character contributes (for example, Cliff shows us Olive's caring big sister side).

4. Chapter and content

Objective
To summarise the main ideas drawn from more than one paragraph.

What you need
Copies of *Letters from the Lighthouse*, images of World War II government posters, photocopiable page 47 'Chapter and content'.

Cross-curricular link
History

What to do
- Review the chapter titles, reminding the children that the author has used slogans from Second World War government campaigns.

- Discuss the function of chapter titles before they begin (to give readers an idea of the content without giving away too much of the plot, and to act as a hook to make them want to read on).

- Tell the children they are going to discuss the purpose behind the slogans. Arrange them into small groups and assign them one of the slogan chapter titles and accompanying poster for discussion. Allow them time to discuss then bring the class back together. Invite volunteers from each group to explain the purpose of the slogan and why it would have been used during World War II.

- Provide pairs with photocopiable page 47 'Chapter and content'. Explain that they should write down the meaning of each government slogan then briefly explain how it relates to the novel – for example, 'Mothers: send them out of London' encouraged families to evacuate their children: in the novel, Olive and Cliff are evacuees.

- Bring the class back together to share ideas. Invite children to reflect how the titles add to the novel.

Differentiation
Support: Discuss the meaning and purpose of the slogans as a class before they complete the photocopiable page.

Extension: Let pairs choose further chapter title slogans to explain and link to the story.

5. Talk about WWII

Objective
To maintain attention and participate actively in collaborative conversations, staying on topic and initiating and responding to comments.

What you need
Copies of *Letters from the Lighthouse*.

Cross-curricular links
History, PSHE

What to do

- Tell the children they are going to consider what the novel has taught them about World War II. Arrange them into small groups and let them discuss all the facts they have learned about the war: when it happened; who was fighting and why; how Britain was attacked; what happened to families in London and also to refugees in German-occupied countries and so on.

- Bring the class back together and invite volunteers from groups to cite facts they have learned. Encourage the children to use correct terminology wherever possible: for example, the 'Luftwaffe' for Nazi planes that bombed British cities; 'air-raid wardens' who were responsible for getting people into shelters during bombing raids.

- Reflect how historical fiction can help us learn about real events. Encourage children to speculate on and discuss the difference between learning facts about the war from non-fiction books or documentary films, and from fictional novels set in the war. If they have read other Second World War novels, encourage them to consolidate information they have learned.

Differentiation
Support: Provide a list of key questions about World War II and challenge children to discuss what we can learn from the novel to answer them.

Extension: Let groups compile a list of facts they have learned about the war from the novel and expand it using their own research.

6. Wartime diaries

Objective
To identify the audience for and purpose of the writing, selecting the appropriate form and using other similar writing as models for their own.

What you need
Copies of *Letters from the Lighthouse*.

Cross-curricular link
PSHE

What to do

- Remind the children of the diary entry they wrote for Olive (Get writing). Encourage discussion on why keeping a diary might be helpful or useful: to record memories, to 'confide' private thoughts and feelings and perhaps to help work through difficult thoughts or feelings?

- Arrange the class into groups of three. Tell them they are going to draft diary entries for the moment when Esther discovers the secret code and the girls begin to fight. Each will write the diary from a different perspective: Olive's, Cliff's or Esther's.

- Ask children to re-read the episode from 'Something was happening upstairs' (towards the end of the chapter 'Loose lips sink ships') to 'Don't you… EVER touch my brother again' (in the following chapter, 'Attack on all fronts'). They should consider how their character is feeling, why they act as they do, and how they feel at the end of the episode.

- When they have drafted their entries, they should compare and contrast them with their writing partners' and discuss how the children each feel about the fight and why.

Differentiation
Support: Read the episode together first and discuss how each character is feeling and why they act as they do.

Extension: Let groups choose another episode featuring three or more characters and repeat the exercise.

Chapter and content

- For each slogan, explain what it means and how it relates to the story.

Government slogan	What the slogan means	How it relates to the story
KEEP CALM AND **CARRY ON**		
MOTHERS: Send them out of London		
CARING FOR EVACUEES IS A NATIONAL SERVICE		
CARELESS TALK COSTS LIVES		
Hitler will send no warning		
UNITED WE ARE STRONGER		

Available in this series:

978-1407-15879-2

978-1407-14224-1

978-1407-16063-4

978-1407-16056-6

978-1407-14228-9

978-1407-16069-6

978-1407-16070-2

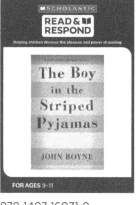

978-1407-16071-9

978-1407-14230-2

978-1407-16057-3

978-1407-16064-1

978-1407-14223-4

978-0702-30890-1

978-0702-30859-8

To find out more,
visit www.scholastic.co.uk/read-and-respond